DIE DEUTSCHE INFORMATIONSBIBLIOTHEK PJÖNGJANG
THE GERMAN LIBRARY PYONGYANG

Sara van der Heide, December 2015

This year marks the twenty-fifth anniversary of the unification treaty between East Germany and West Germany. Today, Korea is still divided in two: North Korea and South Korea.

"Wir wagen ein Experiment, denn wir wollen als Erste dabei sein, wenn Ihr Land beginnt, sich zu öffnen." (We are undertaking a risky experiment, because we want to be the first ones there when your country opens up.)

① With these words Jutta Limbach, the former president of the Goethe-Institut, opened the Office for German Academic and Technical Publishing at the Goethe-Institut's Information Centre Pyongyang, in secluded communist North Korea on June 2, 2004. This extraordinary initiative was perhaps bound to fail, and eventually the library would exist for no more than five years. The library's contents were negotiated over a two-year period, with the North Korean government pressing for academic literature on science, technology, and medicine, while the Goethe-Institut maintained that 50 percent of the books should pertain to German culture, language, literature, and music. The Goethe-Institut not only believed that Germany could be an example for Korea in the unification process, but also that through Germany could contribute to an eventual uniting of the two Koreas.

Due to North Korea's reclusive politics, its communication with South Korea is scarce. For example, there is intranet within North Korea, but no internet connection with the rest of the world. Therefore, today's understanding of North Korea is deeply influenced by foreign powers and especially by the United States. Currently, the United States of America still holds a military base in South Korea, while Korea's history is marked by foreign rule and especially by the colonization by Japan. After decades of Japanese occupation, the Korean War started, which in North Korea is referred to as "The Fatherland Liberation War"; in China the conflict is officially called "the War to Resist Aggression from the United States of America and Aid Korea." Kim Il Sung, the first leader of North Korea, was one of the leaders in fighting against Japanese occupation and US influence. Pride in its autonomy and resistance towards US influence are still the major pillars of North Korean society today.

During the 5th Guangzhou Triennial the Deutsche Informationsbibliothek in Guangzhou (China), affiliated with the Goethe-Insitut, *becomes* the "Deutsche Informationsbibliothek Pjöngjang (Nordkorea)." This intervention is an imaginary transformation of the current geography of the existing library. Under this umbrella a set of cultural activities is offered to the audience, just as a Goethe-Institut usually operates. This time, it includes a reflection on the library itself and the historical context of the reading room, and looks into the possible parallel histories between the two Koreas and the formerly divided Germany.

This project does not claim to find answers to complex political matters, and hopes to succeed in staying away from the usual imagery about North Korea. What this project does aim to do is to have a critical look at national cultural policy and the use of soft power in general, which in this case stems from a Eurocentric capitalistic narrative and perhaps confirms the unequal relation between giver and receiver. What does it mean today in a postcolonial era to open a German reading library in a communist country? What role can art and

"

language play in unlearning the agonistic
opposites and finding new bridges? The
room offers a space for critical questions,
but functions as well as a space for
transcending thinking along the lines of
the nation-state, language, and geography.

During the triennial the library visitor can
find several artworks in the bookshelves.
Books are artworks and artworks are
books. In the library and during the seminar
one can find responses and contributions
from a company of artists from different
generations coming from, amongst others,
Germany, China, and North and South Korea.

On December 13, 2015 there will be a
seminar with cooking performances, music,
talks, and screenings.

[1] A significant part (more than one-
fifth) of the Federal Foreign Office
budget for 2013, of around 800 million
euros, was spent on cultivating cultural
relations abroad. Since WWII, Germany
started to work actively on promoting
a positive image across the globe and
opened 160 Goethe-Institutes—cultural
institutes offering German culture and
language—in ninety-six countries. Since
2004, China has established around 500
Confucius Institutes—Chinese learning
centers—abroad, funded by the Chinese
government.

TIMELY MEDITATIONS

Henk Slager, chief curator
1st Asia Biennial / 5th Guangzhou Triennial

In 1876 the German philosopher Nietzsche stressed in his groundbreaking essay "Untimely Meditations," that—after half a century of historical thinking and the invention of the discipline named "history"—it was exceedingly urgent to reconsider all related cultural values and the rhetorical role of historical constructs and understanding.

He was, however, very well aware of his wrong timing. The nineteenth century was the era in which the spirit—as legitimized in philosopher Hegel's *Phenomenology of Spirit*—manifested itself as a World Spirit; an era also of a Eurocentric attitude completely overlooking the values and qualities of other continents such as Asia.

In the following century, a globalizing thinking about time would manifest itself in new organizational structures such as the nationstate, empire, and capitalism: unifying forces that would pay little attention to how a different sense of time and subjectivity further developed meanwhile in Asia.

It is this negligence, this willful denial of the difference, which is the timely starting point for the fifth Guangzhou Triennial/first Asia Biennial. Its narrative focuses on a paradoxicality that is intrinsically linked to time as described by the Korean philosopher Byungchul Han in *Fatigue Society*, namely that of Western, global, or "World Time" (the perspective of acceleration, speed, visibility, exhaustion, a transgressive/progressive modernity, ultra-capitalism, knowledge production, and economy) versus Asian time (the perspective of tranquility, reflection, concentration, various forms of modernity, and emphasis on values and wisdom). Starting from this insight, the Guangzhou Triennial intends to be a critical catalyst for querying the current "World Time standard" —not for the sake of replacing it with another form of time, but with the attempt to end the self-centered, exclusive, and expansionistic logic that presents itself universally and seems to be intrinsically linked to it.

This impossibility of universality is at the core of Sara van der Heide's project *Die Deutsche Informationsbibliothek Pjöngjang— The German Library Pyongyang* (2015). The project—that takes place on site at the Sun Yat-sen Library—analyzes the cultural politics developed by the Goethe-Institut on the basis of its temporary branch opened about ten years ago in the North Korean capital. In the name of Goethe—who was probably the last *homo universalis* history has known—the institute wanted to introduce visitors to perspectives and values presented as universal.

Sara van der Heide's project is a layered approach of the issues mentioned above and consists of, among other things, interventions, collaborations with other artists and designers (such as Hans Haacke, Sora Kim, and Chen Tong), and a parallel seminar program (with Louwrien Wijers, Chankyong Park, Stefan Dreyer, among others). The project should not only be viewed as a historical reconstruction, but above all as a space for imagination and critical reflection (with regards to the expansionist "soft power" politics), that takes the relativity and historicity of cultural values as its starting point.

Sara van der Heide, *The Library Database from the Goethe-Institut Library and Information Center (2004–09) from Pyongyang*

2015, in collaboration with Dongyoung Lee, and Kristian Johansen
digital library database and 5,000 library index cards

The original idea was to ship the books and other media from the former Pyongyang reading room to Guangzhou. But the Goethe-Institut Seoul has informed me that the original books and other media were distributed over several parts of Asia, for example to Mongolia, medical centers in Pyongyang, and other places. What is present in Guangzhou is the database of the media—5,000 books, DVDs, and CDs—that were shipped to Pyongyang in 2004. All books, films, and music are categorized by subject and can be searched by tag/alphabet/author/subject/index-number. The selection of the books illustrates the different interests of Germany and North Korea. The library's contents were negotiated over a two-year period, with the North Korean government pressing for academic literature on science, technology, and medicine, while the Goethe-Institut maintained that 50 percent of the books should pertain to German culture, language, literature, and music.

Changho Choi, *Mountain Paekdu in Spring*

2004, printed textile banners

The painted landscape of Chonji (The Heaven Lake) is visible on two banners hanging in the library. The peak of the mountain Paekdu is considered "the Sacred Mountain of Revolution" in North Korea. Choi's brushwork is in the Mongol style, which shapes figures by coloring without preliminary contours. The area and the mountain are known for two reasons: as a base for guerilla battles against the Japanese, who occupied the Korean peninsula for decades, and because Koreans consider Paekdu one of the three sacred mountains and a place of their ancestral origin.

Conversation Pieces between Erich Honecker and Kim Il Sung

2015, published by Back to the Mountain Publishing House,
on the occasion of *The German Library Pyongyang* (2015)

On the shelves of the German Library, in the section about the Cold War,
you can find a publication with two documents from the 1970s that show
an exchange between the former leaders of the former German Democratic
Republic and Democratic People's Republic of Korea: Erich Honecker and Kim
Il Sung, respectively. The two documents embody the historical friendship
pact between the DPRK and the GDR (a pact that also included China)
that resulted in a long-term relationship and cultural exchange between
East Germany and North Korea. This friendship made it eventually possible
to open a German library and information center in Pyongyang. The letters
show the strong desire, from the side of the North Koreans for unification
without US influence.

Sara van der Heide, *Johann Wolfgang von Goethe Has a House in 169 Places*

2015, 169 business cards, displayed in alphabetical order

The Goethe-Institut has 169 institutions across the world promoting German
language and culture, funded by the Federal Republic of Germany. On 169
individual business cards, the Goethe-Institut's namesake, Johann Wolfgang
von Goethe (1749–1832), is printed together with the address of each of the
Goethe Institutes around the globe. These familiar objects offer an alter-
native means of mapping the ubiquity and lingering imperial implications of
national-cultural institutes in a globalized terrain. The business cards show
the person Johann Wolfgang von Goethe embodied: a poet, a politician,
a scientist, a playwright, and a novelist.

Hans Haacke, *Die Freiheit wird jetzt einfach gesponsert – aus der Portokasse (Freedom Is Now Simply Going to be Sponsored—Out of Petty Cash)*

1990, four photographs

In 1990, Giovanni Anselmo, Barbara Bloom, Christian Boltanski, Hans
Haacke, Rebecca Horn, Ilya Kabakov, Jannis Kounellis, Via Lewandowski,
Mario Merz, Raffael Rheinsberg, and Krzysztof Wodiczko were invited to
produce a temporary public installation consisting of complementary parts
in each of the two sections of the still-divided city of Berlin. The exhibition,
financed by the city of West Berlin, opened several months before the
unification of the city and Germany. Its title, *The Finiteness of Freedom,*

was coined by Heiner Müller, a well-known East German dramatist, poet, writer, and theater director. In 1961, twenty-nine years earlier, the GDR (East Germany) had carved out a heavily patrolled, barren stretch of land along the border with West Berlin delineated by unscalable walls, electrified fences, and minefields. About 175 people trying to escape to the West died in what became known as the "death strip."

A watchtower near the Heinrich-Heine-Strasse checkpoint was chosen for the project. Its windows were newly fitted with tinted glass, reminiscent of the "Palasthotel" in East Berlin, a luxurious guesthouse of the GDR. The searchlight on the roof was replaced by a slowly rotating Mercedes star—since 1965 a giant Mercedes star had been revolving on top of the "Europa Center," the tallest building in the heart of the fashionable shopping district of West Berlin.

Two inscriptions in bronze letters were mounted on opposite sides of the watchtower. They were quotes by famous people that had been used in a series of advertisements by Daimler-Benz. One of the quotes, *"Bereit sein ist alles"* ("the readiness is all") by Shakespeare, echoes "Be prepared—always prepared," the motto of the Young Pioneers, the GDR's youth organization. The other, *"Kunst bleibt Kunst"* by Goethe, translated as "Art will always remain art," had been used in Mercedes ads in *The New York Times*.

A few months before the exhibition, Daimler-Benz bought a large piece of empty land at Potsdamer Platz, a site near the wall that had been the old center of Berlin and was expected to become its hub again. The city of Berlin sold the tract to Daimler-Benz before an urban plan for the newly opened areas had been developed. The company paid one-tenth of the estimated market price.

Daimler-Benz is among those members of the German industries that had vigorously promoted Hitler's rise to power. Its chairman and its president were both members of the SS. Like other companies during the war, Daimler-Benz relied extensively on forced labor.

The company prospered again after the war. It is the largest enterprise in Germany and is also the largest producer of war material. In spite of an international arms embargo, the company supplied the South African apartheid regime's military and police with more than 6,000 vehicles, including rocket launchers. During the 1980s, Daimler-Benz sold helicopters, military vehicles, and missiles to Saddam Hussein.

Daimler-Benz has been a conspicuous sponsor of art exhibitions. In 1986, it commissioned Andy Warhol to make a series of paintings of its cars from the beginning up to the 1980s. They were exhibited posthumously in 1988 at the Guggenheim Museum—sponsored by Mercedes.

Sora Kim, *Abstract Reading*

2015, printed text

In the German Library there are books present on German culture, history,
philosophy, science, German foreign relations policy, the Cold War, and
WWII as well as literature and music scores. A random selection of pages
from different books was sent to Sora Kim, who is based in Seoul. From
these pages she recreates a new text: text beyond meaning and different
languages. Her abstract writing gives voice to a language far from the
conventional notion of communication and logical thinking. Her work gives
new meaning to the usage of the library and its books and offers an
analogy for the current transformation of the library.

Chen Tong, *The True Bookcase*

2015, bookcase and video

Will bookcases still exist in the future? Making a "true" bookcase is as
important as thinking about the value of thought. This bookcase is not
a decoration. In the process of producing it, we only consider its bearing
capacity since the thought itself has weight. During the public dialogue,
we will discuss what kinds of books we should put on the bookcase. At the
same time, the public will know the production process of a true bookcase.

Künstlerinnengruppe Erfurt (The Women Artist Group Erfurt), *Fashion for Women by Women Fashion-Object-Show* by Gabriele Stötzer

original 8mm film, 8 min
courtesy of Irmgard Senf

Gabriele Stötzer was one of the founders of the Künstlerinnengruppe Erfurt during the '80s in the GDR. The group made paintings, weavings, pottery, and 8mm films and later started to hold several performances in churches in Erfurt. The women were looking for ways to express themselves individually in a controlled society, dominated by men. The women artists could only perform in private spaces or in churches. This video shows a fashion-object-show in the Augustine monastery in Erfurt. People were making self-made outfits. Gabriele Stötzer: "This was art for everybody, with an egalitarian, democratic approach. That kind of fashion was not exclusive, but accessible." For the show they were looking for models—normal women, not the women seen in fashion magazines—and many women responded to it.

Janet Grau, *Rückblick/Re-viewing*

2003, video, 23 min

Rückblick/Re-Viewing shows a total of thirty people describing paintings. This multi-part installation is based on video material that was filmed in the depot of the Kunstfonds des Freistaates Sachsen (State Art Fund of Saxony). Once belonging to the Büro für Bildende Kunst des Rates des Bezirkes Dresden, an official visual arts institution in the former East Germany, the artworks that were used are now part of the Kunstfonds collection. From amongst the over 21,000 works of the collection, Janet Grau chose fifteen pictures, which were then presented to the *Rückblick/Re-Viewing* participants. Before seeing the selection of pictures, those invited to participate neither knew what sort of paintings they would be faced with, nor did they know that these would be images from the former GDR. Over the course of several days, the participants came one by one to the depot, where they each selected "their" picture. They were not told which paintings the others had chosen, nor did they receive information regarding the artworks (such as artist's name, title of the work, date, etc.). Grau asked them each to describe their chosen work of art to her, but provided no guidelines as to how the artworks should be described. The picture itself remains concealed from the camera as well as the audience—only the backside of the painting is visible. The video material invites us to observe the speakers, their gestures, their searching gaze, and their moments of discomfort. We are witness to their struggle to capture the picture in words. Instead of a debate concerning political contexts for art or questions regarding its value, we observe intimate, individual encounters with paintings. The question of the quality of these works remains unanswered—that is, neither negative nor positive assumptions are made, as has often been the case when works of the socialist realism period are shown. Instead, the focus is on the dynamics of viewing art itself as well as the attempt to capture this experience in words. The image is reflected in the faces, words, and attitudes of the participants, but remains hidden from view in the final installation. We have only an empty backside, an ironic commentary on the absence of these images in the public realm.

Chankyong Park, *Flying*

2005, video, 13 min

In June 2000, the first North-South summit after the Korean War took place. This film is edited from TV sources recording the flights from South Korea via Pyongyang, the airport, and the streets of Pyongyang. The video's soundtrack is taken from the beginning of Isang Yun's 1977 composition "Double Concerto," which was inspired by the myth of Gyeonu and Jiknyeo. According to the myth, the King of Heaven punishes the couple's lack of diligence by stranding one of them on a star in the west and the other on a star in the east. However, the couple succeeds in reuniting for one day a year, on July 7, when birds who took pity on them built a bridge across the Milky Way. Yun compared the myth to North-South relations. The distance between North and South is as far as the distance across the Milky Way. The encounter of Gyeonu and Jiknyeo symbolizes reunification. Yun, when he composed the piece, may have been imagining the infinite number of birds needed to build a bridge spanning the galaxy. Unable to return to his divided oountry, Yun died an exile—in a newly reunified Germany, no less.

Chankyong Park, *Blackout*

2009, video, 3:50 min

In North Korea, "Joseon painting" is a genre of painting that depicts forceful seas and waves. The "revolutionary romanticism" of these paint-ings brings to mind the chronic insufficiency of energy in North Korea. The "national forms" of these paintings remind me of the giant power plants from the West investigating the potential for exploitation of oil and gas in the North Korean Sea. The Joseon painters of the Mansudae Art Studio perfectly serve their political role in North Korea. Chankyong Park's "video art" appropriates their art and wastes the electricity.

1 "Waves of Haegumgang": *Study of Wave Shapes from Joseon Painting,* by Sunggeun Kim, published 2003 in North Korea by 2.16 Art Education Publishing, contains sixty photo images of wave paintings. In this book, the way of painting the sea and waves as "Joseon Painting" is explained in detail over 120 pages.

2 In 2000, hydroelectric power plants generated about 67 percent of
North Korea's electricity. As a result of the electricity shortage, North
Korea has resorted to a rationing system. The country often experiences
blackouts for extended periods of time, and frequent power losses due
to an antiquated transmission grid.

3 At present (2002), South Korea has not agreed to supply the North with
electricity from its own transmission grid. North Korea also has reportedly
discussed the possibility of electricity aid with Russia.

4 As it is considered to be a geological extension of China's Bohai Bay,
the West Korea Bay of North Korea may contain hydrocarbon reserves.
Corporations such as Sweden's Taurus Energy AB, Britain's Soco
International, and Aminex PLC are investigating the potential for
exploitation of oil and gas in the North Korean sea.

Liu Ding, *Gift (2)*

2011, video, 2:51 min

This was a birthday gift commissioned by a collector for her own birthday
that appears in the form of a three-screen video installation. I took the
clip of Marilyn Monroe singing "Happy Birthday" to President Kennedy at
his birthday party in 1962, cut it into fragments and inserted between
her singing my own writings about having dreams and expectations in life.
These are the writings I put down to intersect Monroe's singing:

For some people, dreaming is an everyday practice, an internal
program, a natural way of being / Imagining a position other than
the one that they are already in / Anticipating being in a position
other than the one that they are already in / Longing for a situation
other than one that they are already in.

Kyungman Kim, *Long Live His Majesty*

2002, HD video, 13 min

Daehan News was the name of a propaganda film series made by the
Korean government press from 1952 to 1994. During this time, *Daehan
News* produced one film clip per week. *Long Live His Majesty* is a sampling
of the *Daehan News* series from 1952 to 1960. *Long Live His Majesty* is
about dictator Syngman Rhee, who was the first president of South Korea.
He appears in this film as the man for whom every day is celebrated as a
birthday. If the United States defines North Korea as a dictatorial country
of totalitarian insanity, this is due not to a misunderstanding of North
Korea, but by a misunderstanding of the United States. If the majority of
Americans knew what has happened this last century, like how the US
government has supported war crimes and dictatorships, maybe they may
find it difficult to talk about North Korea in this way. Likewise, when South

Korea defines North Korea as a one-man-worshipping, totalitarian society, they cannot avoid a certain irony: that during the last several decades, South Korea was absolutely a country run by several one-man dictatorships. South Korea has been in the same situation as North Korea except for one thing—the tyrant has changed several times. The fact that people have shown such hostility to North Korea and have at one point worshipped a tyrant such as President Rhee as "Our Great Father," is ironic.

09.30–10.00	Doors open
10.00–10.15	Opening of the seminar: *Complete, Embrace* A song composed by Rory Pilgrim, performed by Robyn Haddon (Voice), Xiaojuan Xing (Cello), Long Liu (Sheng)
10.15–10.30	Opening word: Gabriele Gauler, director of the Goethe-Institut Hong Kong
10.30–12.30	Open conversation on the German Reading Room in Pyongyang; German culture, music, and books as a means for reunification between North and South Korea Speakers: • Stefan Dreyer, director of the Goethe-Institut Seoul • Chankyong Park, artist and filmmaker • Kyungman Kim, filmmaker • Gabriele Stötzer / Künstlerinnengruppe Erfurt, from the former GDR • Moderator: Hyunjin Kim
12.30–14.00	(Lunch break) Cooking performance: *Blissful Peace Soup* Egon Hanfstingl
14.00–15.30	Lecture *Goethe and His Food: the Influence of China on Goethe* Louwrien Wijers (Short break)
15.45–16.15	Performance-lecture on *The True Bookcase* Chen Tong
16.15–16.45	A reading performance: *Abstract Reading* written by Sora Kim, read by four performers in Korean, German, Chinese, and English
16.45–17.00	Closing of the seminar: *Complete, Embrace* A song composed by Rory Pilgrim, performed by Robyn Haddon (Voice), Xiaojuan Xing (Cello), Long Liu (Sheng)

독일문화원

Opening of the seminar: *Complete, Embrace*
A song composed by Rory Pilgrim, performed by
Robyn Haddon (Voice), Xiaojuan Xing (Cello), Long Liu (Sheng)

For the seminar, artist Rory Pilgrim composes a song that will open and close the day. Broken into two parts, the song attempts to encapsulate one of the most primal human instincts—to embrace. An instinct that unites humans, from the beginning of a new life to the reunion of those once separated. Trying to deal with the complexity of reunification and pain of separation, Pilgrim reflects on the possibility of the human voice. As a fundamental instrument that we share, Pilgrim draws upon the potential of the voice to unite us and express our human experience. As an instrument, the voice is a direct channel for our words through which we can transform our emotional understanding of them. Collaborating with the British singer and artist Robyn Haddon, Pilgrim composes a new piece of music exploring words of love, harmony, peace, pain, and loss to consider how the very personal can resonate universally. Working with local musicians, the voice weaves with the wordless melodies of their instruments, uniting people beyond the comprehension of language.

Opening word: Gabriele Gauler,
director Goethe-Institut Hong Kong

Open conversation on *The German Reading Room
in Pyongyang*; German Music and Books as a Means
For Reunification between North and South Korea

Part 1 presentations—75 minutes

Speakers:
- Stefan Dreyer, the director Goethe-Institut Seoul, will speak about the process and the reasoning behind the opening of a German library in Pyongyang. Further, he will talk about the current German cultural activities in Pyongyang and North Korea.
- Chankyong Park, artist and filmmaker from South Korea, will present his works *Black Out* and *Flying*, which are also shown in the video program. He will talk about his practice reflecting on the Cold War and his works addressing the relations between North and South Korea.
- Kyungman Kim, filmmaker, will give a short introduction of his work and how the dictatorship in South Korea blocked the formation of the labor movement.
- Gabriele Stötzer / Künstlerinnengruppe Erfurt, artist, will give a short introduction of her practice and she will speak about her collective performances with the women's artist group in the GDR and her role in the peaceful unification movement in the '80s in Germany.

- Moderator, Hyunjin Kim, curator and writer will reflect on the presence of foreign cultural organizations in South Korea.

Short break—15 minutes

Part 2 open conversation with participants
Moderated by Hyunjin Kim—45 minutes

Underlying topics and questions are: Can Germany's own history help in the possible reunification process between North and South Korea? Both divided into two; influenced by the United States on one side and on the other side by the communistic countries. Or is the parallel too simplistic, looking into the very different histories of both countries? How to place Germany's presence in a larger framework of Western imperialism and self aclaimed eurocentric thinking? What are the motives for Germany to open worldwide (and in North Korea) German cultural centers after WWII? Political economical motives? What were/are the possible effects of the German reading room in Pyongyang? And is the image of a secluded North Korea and a German safe haven possibly too simplistic? Can the German reading room contribute to the unification process?

Cooking performance: *Blissful Peace Soup*
Egon Hanfstingl

Egon Hanfstingl, chef and artist, will execute his *Blissful Peace Soup* performance in Guangzhou. This soup speaks through a direct and universal language without words: through the stomach. The ingredients and the aromas permeates in each cell inside of each of us. The ingredients for his soup will be both local and from around Europe and Asia. One ancient Chinese dietary text Egon refers to in the making of the soup comes from Sun Simiao's (621–713) "Prescriptions Worth a Thousand Gold," which was completed in the 650s, during the Tang dynasty.

Lecture: *Goethe And His Food: the Influence of China on Goethe*,
Louwrien Wijers

Louwrien Wijers, artist and writer, has mainly produced "mental sculptures" over the last decades. Her aim is to introduce subtle changes in our consciousness by dialogue and intensively speaking together. In Guangzhou at the Goethe-Institut, she proposes to exchange thoughts on the influence of China on the namesake of the German national cultural institute: Johann Wolfgang von Goethe. In 1809 Julius Klaproth (1783–1853), the intern of Goethe, published an overview of Chinese literature. Also, Goethe followed the macrobiotic diet of his doctor W.C. Hufeland (1762–1836), published in 1797, into which Hufeland inserted knowledge from China on the working of food on the body. He called his approach "soft healing," using nature's powers to prolong life in contrast to the "heroic medical science." From

these two sources Goethe was influenced by China. Restoring the Eurasian
culture is here the aim of Louwrien Wijers.

Performance-lecture: *The True Bookcase*
Chen Tong

Reading performance: *Abstract Reading*
Written by Sora Kim, read by four performers in Korean,
German, Chinese, and English

In the German library there are books on German culture, history,
philosophy, science, German foreign policy, the Cold War, and WWII, but
also literature and music scores. A random selection of pages from different
books was sent to Sora Kim, who is based in Seoul. From these pages
Sora Kim recreated a new text: text beyond meaning and the different
languages. *Abstract Reading* is about an impossible language, yet the most
evolved and genuine type. When reading in this language the word instantly
fades away, never to be repeated ever again, not even by the same reader.
The pronounciation of a word varies in great range depending on the reader
and depending on every detailed moment the reader was/is facing. Its
pronounciation is possible only from the most sincere and truthful reading.
Meaning in this language is never in a fixed form but is still perfectly
sharable in an indescrible way of understanding.

Closing of the seminar: *Complete, Embrace*
A song composed by Rory Pilgrim, performed by
Robyn Haddon (Voice), Xiaojuan Xing (Cello), Long Liu (Sheng)

SHORT BIOGRAPHIES OF THE CONTRIBUTORS

Chankyong Park born in 1965, Seoul,
South Korea; lives in Seoul, South Korea
Artist, filmmaker

Changho Choi born 1960, Onseong, North Korea;
lives in Pyongyang, North Korea
Artist, chief of Mansudae Art Studio Pyongyang

Chen Tong born in 1962, Hunan Province, China;
lives in Guangzhou, China
Artist, founder Borges Libreria Institute for
Contemporary Art, Guangzhou

Ding Liu born in 1976, Changzhou, China;
lives in Beijing, China
Artist

Dongyoung Lee born in 1981, Daegu, South
Korea; lives in Amsterdam, the Netherlands
Designer

Egon Hanfstingl born in 1960, Hilden, Germany;
lives in Hallum, the Netherlands
Artist, chef

Gabriele Gauler Germany; lives in Hong Kong
Director Goethe-Institut Hong Kong

Gabriele Stötzer / Künstlerinnengruppe Erfurt
born in 1953, Erleben, Germany; lives in Erfurt,
Germany
Artist, co-founder Künstlerinnengruppe Erfurt

Hans Haacke born in 1936, Cologne,
Germany; lives in New York City, United States
Artist

Hyunjin Kim born in 1975, Daejon, South Korea;
lives in Seoul, South Korea
Author, curator

Janet Grau born in 1964, Cleveland, United
States, lives in Heidelberg, Germany
Artist

Kristian Johansen born 1987, Copenhagen,
Denmark; lives in London, United Kingdom
Webdesigner

Kyungman Kim born in 1972, Seoul, South Korea;
lives in Seoul, South Korea
Filmmaker

Long Liu born in 1981, Shandong province,
China; lives in Guangzhou, China
Sheng player

Louwrien Wijers born in 1941, Aalten, the
Netherlands; lives in Ferwert, the Netherlands
Artist, writer

Robyn Haddon born in 1992, St. Albans, United
Kingdom; lives in Sheffield, United Kingdom
Singer

Rory Pilgrim born in 1988, Bristol, United
Kingdom; lives in Amsterdam, the Netherlands
Artist, composer

Sara van der Heide born in 1977, Busan,
South Korea; lives in Amsterdam,
the Netherlands
Artist

Sora Kim born in 1965, Seoul, South Korea;
lives in Seoul, South Korea
Artist

Stefan Dreyer born in 1958, Singen, Germany;
lives in Seoul, South Korea
Director Goethe-Institut Seoul

Xiaojuan Xing born in 1990, Hainan province,
China; lives in Guangzhou, China
Cello player